Ann
Bancroft

Ann Bancroft

On Top of the World

Dorothy Wenzel

DILLON PRESS, INC.
Minneapolis, Minnesota 55415

Photographic Acknowledgments

The photographs are reproduced through the courtesy of Ann Bancroft (page 50), Bob Firth (pages 36, 54, and cover), Jim Gasparini (page 52), and Will Steger (pages 8, 11, 42, 45, 48)/Firth Photo Bank; Dick Bancroft; Tim Elgren (pages 30-31, 33); Kvasnik (page 27); Ruby Loos (page 14, bottom); and Saint James School.

Library of Congress Cataloging-in-Publication Data

Wenzel, Dorothy.
    Ann Bancroft : on top of the world / Dorothy Wenzel.
        p.   cm. — (Taking part)
    Bibliography: p.
    Includes index.
    Summary: Covers the life and exploits of the first woman to reach the North Pole by dogsled.
    ISBN 0-87518-418-9 : $9.95

1. Bancroft, Ann—Journeys—Juvenile literature.   2. North Pole—Juvenile literature.   [1. Bancroft, Ann.   2. Adventure and adventurers.]   I. Title.
G627.W46   1990
910'.91632—dc20
[B]
[92]   89-11980
                                                                   CIP
                                                                    AC

Dillon Press, Inc., 242 Portland Avenue South
Minneapolis, Minnesota 55415

Printed in the United States of America
1 2 3 4 5 6 7 8 9 10 99 98 97 96 95 94 93 92 91 90

Contents

Ann Bancroft

When Ann Bancroft reached the North Pole on May 1, 1986, she became the first woman to travel to the Pole by dogsled over the arctic ice. She also became a role model for young women, and for young people with disabilities in particular. As a child Ann learned that she suffered from dyslexia, a condition that made reading and learning in school very difficult for her. Despite her disability, she graduated from high school and college, and worked as a physical education teacher and athletic director for schools in Saint Paul and Minneapolis, Minnesota. She also developed skills as an athlete, a camper and wilderness explorer, and a mountain climber.

Ann Bancroft was the only woman asked to join Will Steger's team for the 1986 international polar expedition. "If you have one woman with seven men, the woman has to be special," said Steger at the time. During the fifty-five-day journey to the North Pole, Ann proved that she was, indeed, special and carried out her duties under the most extreme conditions. When all the reporters flew to the Pole to join the victorious Steger team, it was Ann who read the team's statement to the world. Ann Bancroft has received many awards and honors since returning to her home in the Twin Cities, and has spoken to groups all over the United States. Still, this brave and determined young woman continues to seek new and different challenges in all areas of her life.

1

Go Ahead and Try

Blinding white light, ice ridges, and patches of deep black water stretched as far as the eye could see. For miles and miles, the barren ice of the Arctic Sea showed no signs of life—no trees, no animals, and no people. Few creatures, however strong, could survive in the howling winds and freezing cold temperatures. The polar ice cap at the top of the world is one of the most difficult and dangerous places to travel.

From high above in a plane, though, a small group of humans and sled dogs could be seen braving the harsh polar sea on their way to the North Pole.

Suddenly Ann Bancroft stumbled upon a wide crack in the ice—a patch of open water called a lead. She wondered how the team of sleds, dogs, and men

Ann Bancroft rides behind a sled during the Steger International Polar Expedition.

would get across this time. Should they make a floating ice bridge? Should they try to jump? Before she could decide, the snowy edge broke away, and Ann plunged into the freezing seawater.

Afraid that the other members of the expedition would accidentally drive over her with the dogsleds, she yelled, "Hey, Paul, I'm over here!" As he approached, she gathered all her strength and pulled herself up onto the ice. Had Ann stayed in the water, she would have died in minutes. Instead, she changed into dry pants and socks and was quickly back on the trail, working hard to stay warm.

Despite the danger of her icy plunge, Ann stayed calm. "It was a good day for a dunk," she said, even though it was -30° F outside. Days passed before Ann stopped shivering, but she rarely complained. Stubborn and courageous, Ann was more determined than ever to make it to the North Pole.

After falling into a lead, Ann quickly changes her wet, icy clothes.

Will Steger had to be very careful when he chose the members of the 1986 Steger International Polar Expedition. Though he hadn't met Ann Bancroft, he had heard good things about her. In 1983 she had saved the life of his friend Tim Elgren while they were climbing Mount McKinley in Alaska. Steger decided to ask this remarkable young woman if she would join his experienced team of explorers.

In her outdoor adventures and as a physical education teacher, Ann had proved herself to be a capable leader. She was athletic, energetic, and had a good sense of humor. Will Steger soon became convinced that thirty-year-old Ann Bancroft would be a valuable member of his expedition.

Ann was thrilled to join the team of seven men and forty-nine sled dogs. If the mission succeeded, she would be the first woman to reach the North Pole by dogsled. The 500-mile journey across the polar sea was the biggest challenge she had ever faced—bigger than her childhood struggle with school, bigger even than her climb up Mount McKinley. Still, she loved adventure, and the more exciting the better.

Shortly after she was born on September 29, 1955, Ann was on the move. To keep her from escaping during nap time, her mother would put a folding divider over her bed. When Ann was a toddler, she would climb her grandmother's bookcase to reach the things on top.

Ann's parents, Richard and Deborah Bancroft, encouraged her courageous spirit. "Go ahead and try," her parents would say, "you might just get what you want."

At the Bancrofts' old farmhouse in Mendota Heights, Minnesota, Ann and her two brothers and two sisters could explore the surrounding acres of

(Top) Ann as a baby with her mother, Deborah Bancroft. (Right) Ann (about two years old) with her brother Bill and Deborah Bancroft.

fields. She liked to pretend she was a pirate building rafts to float down the creek, or an adventurer canoeing in the far north. During the winter she would build snow forts, sleeping shacks, and tunnels.

Ann started school at Somerset Elementary in Mendota Heights. After two years, she transferred to Summit School, a private school in nearby Saint Paul, Minnesota. Ann had a difficult time with reading and spelling because she had a learning disability known as dyslexia. When she tried to read, signals on the nerve paths to her brain would get mixed up, so letters and numbers would seem scrambled. Since her teachers didn't yet know she had dyslexia, they weren't able to explain why learning was so hard for her.

Ann was tutored to help her through her schoolwork, but she dreaded these lessons. "Tutoring was a horrible experience for me," she recalled. "I remem-

Ann (top row, left) with second-grade classmates at Summit School.

ber hiding behind the door waiting for this lady to come and get me." The only parts of school she liked were recess and gym class. Ann was a natural athlete, and these periods were the only times when she felt good about herself.

When Ann was ten years old, her father quit his

In this family photograph, taken shortly before the Bancrofts left for Kenya, ten-year-old Ann is at the left.

job as an insurance agent, and he and Deborah Bancroft decided to take the family to Africa. Dick Bancroft had long been interested in helping people from other countries. He wanted some firsthand experience to gain an understanding of other cultures, and he felt that working for the church as a missionary

In Kenya, Ann learned many new things from her African friends.

might be the best way to do that. Ann was excited about the prospect of a new adventure in a faraway land.

Although life in Kenya was not at all like growing up in Minnesota, Ann enjoyed the new experiences. She learned from her British and African friends

Wild animals such as this giraffe roamed freely near the Bancrofts' home in Kenya.

about how people from other lands viewed the world. They told her that Kenya had just fought a revolution and had won its independence from Great Britain. Later, Ann recalled what this time meant to her. "Being in another culture like Kenya gives you a thirst to want to know what's out there. Not everything revolves around the United States. Our way isn't always the best way."

For Ann, one of the best parts about living in Africa was the animals. The Bancrofts had chosen a house in the red, rolling hills of the country, where animals roamed freely. Some of Ann's pets were more unusual than her Minnesota pets. She had two bush babies that could climb walls, a dormouse that she kept in the pocket of her school uniform, two kinds of antelopes, and a monkey named Malcolm.

After two years in Africa, the Bancrofts returned to Minnesota. Ann didn't want to go home—she

Ann (second row from top, middle) *with seventh-grade classmates.*

loved Kenya and wanted to spend the rest of her life there.

By this time, Ann was in seventh grade, and her school had merged with the Saint Paul Academy. Classes were even more difficult than she had remembered. Halfway through the year, she was removed from her classes and tested for learning disabilities. This was the first time Ann learned she had dyslexia. Knowing she had a problem, though, didn't make it easier for her. "It was just one more thing where I felt stupid or different," she said.

Despite her hard work with tutors and on her own, Ann had little to show for her efforts. Her teachers suggested that she drop back a grade, but she stubbornly refused. Although she kept trying, she finally left Saint Paul Academy to finish eleventh grade at Sibley High School.

What Ann lacked in her studies, she more than made up for in school sports. When she discovered that Sibley had only track, tennis, and swimming teams for girls, she joined the track team and helped win regional championships. Ann also tried to get the athletic director to organize a basketball team at Sibley. When no one acted, she started her own team and became a coach, referee, and player.

During school vacations, Ann attended Camp Widjiwagan in northern Minnesota. Camping, canoeing, and other adventures delighted her. After her senior year in high school, she went on a two-month canoeing expedition with four young women from the camp.

While she was at the camp, Ann decided to become a counselor and help others learn camping skills. She liked the idea of teaching, and began to think of going to college to get the skills she needed.

After graduating from high school, Ann went on a two-month canoe-ing trip. In college, she enjoyed camping, skiing, and other outdoor activities.

2

Beating the Odds

Although Ann's high school record had not been good, she was determined to give college her best effort. She was ready to attend whatever college accepted her, and the University of Wyoming did. Unfortunately, her canoeing trip after high school caused her to start her classes one semester late. By that time, many of the first-year students had already made friends, and Ann was lonely.

College was a struggle for Ann, who often worried that she would fail. Still, she took comfort in Wyoming's mountains, which provided many opportunities for her to camp and ski. She also played field hockey, basketball, and softball.

After Ann's second year at college, her parents'

house burned down, and she came back to Minnesota to help her family. She also took some time to think about her goals, help a friend who had been in a car accident, and work on a construction project with her brother Bill. That Christmas the Bancrofts returned to Kenya, and Ann and Bill stayed to climb Mount Kenya, one of Africa's highest mountains.

When it came time for Ann to return to college, she did not want to go back to Wyoming. That university had dropped some sports programs that she liked, and she wanted a change. Ann decided to attend another college with mountains nearby and was accepted by the University of Oregon at Eugene.

In Oregon she still struggled to overcome her dyslexia. To graduate from college and find a job as a physical education teacher, Ann had to complete a student teaching program. But her grades were not high enough for her to get in this program. She peti-

At the time this family picture was taken, Ann had both of her feet in casts because she had broken her heels.

tioned again and again, and even repeated some classes to boost her grades. "Why don't you just give up?" suggested faculty members, but Ann would not quit. She worked until her grades were high enough to qualify her as a student teacher.

One of Ann's first duties was to teach physical education to students with cerebral palsy, a form of paralysis that is often caused at or before birth. "There was such a wide range of physical abilities," Ann said, remembering her students. "Some could walk, some could throw a ball, and some had to be strapped to their chairs. That was a real challenge to me, and I adored it. It got me going. I got my minor in special education."

Ann could relate to the students who struggled. Every small step of progress they made meant a lot to her. When she graduated from the University of Oregon with a degree in physical education and a minor in special education, her parents were proud. Determined and stubborn, Ann had beaten the odds, amazing herself, her parents, and the system.

Ann's first job after college was at Saint James School in Saint Paul as the athletic director and physical education teacher. She also developed an afterschool sports program. Ann enjoyed her job, and she inspired the children to accomplish as much as they could. "I wanted my kids to try," she said. "I wanted them to come away with a sense of who they were. The gym time is a time to explore things, take a few risks."

After two years at Saint James School, Ann switched to Clara Barton Open School in Minneapolis. Before she began her new job, however, she took a year off to coach and to work at a mountaineering store. In June 1983, Ann climbed Alaska's Mount McKinley with her friend Tim Elgren. Mount Mc-

Ann climbs up a snowy ridge on Mount McKinley.

Kinley, the highest peak in North America, stands 20,320 feet high and challenges the skills of experienced mountaineers.

Ann and Tim started climbing on June 1, and by June 17 they had reached 18,000 feet, where they made their final tent camp. Early the next morning, they started toward the summit. At eight o'clock that evening, they finally made it to the top. "I couldn't believe it," said Ann. "There were several times on the trip that it was just so hard I didn't think I'd make it."

She was happily taking pictures when Tim said, "We've got to go. I'm just really cold." He started to go down the mountain. Tim knew he had hypothermia, a dangerous condition which causes the body to lose heat faster than it can produce it. As Ann hurried to catch up with him, she could hear him mumbling.

After eighteen days of climbing, Ann Bancroft stands on the summit of Mount McKinley.

"Who are you talking to?" she asked.

"I don't know, they're your friends," said Tim.

Ann knew that Tim was confused and out of control, and that she had to get him down to the base camp safely. With great effort, she managed to climb down the icy slopes with Tim to their tent by midnight. Several more hours passed before he was warm enough to sleep.

The next day Ann and Tim had to climb down the steepest part of the mountain. After further difficulties, including a fall that burned Ann's hand down to the bone, they finally returned safely to their starting point. Later, she described the danger of the adventure. "When doing something risky, things happen, but you work as a team. One day you help him, the next day, he helps you."

Ann's success in helping Tim was no accident. She was prepared for emergencies by her earlier training in first aid and emergency medicine. "The thrill for me in the outdoors," Ann said, "is that you get as prepared as you can and then you go out there. There is always that little element of the unknown. You make decisions that will stick and live with the results."

After the trip, Ann returned to teach at the Clara Barton Open School. Two years later, in 1985, Will Steger asked her to take part in her greatest adventure yet, as a member of his international polar expedition.

3

Getting Ready

Ann, eager for a new challenge, was excited about the trip to the Pole. Will Steger wanted his team to make the first confirmed journey to the North Pole by dogsled and skis, carrying all its own equipment, and without accepting supplies from the outside. He had sought support for the expedition from the National Geographic Society and other groups.

As Ann said, "There aren't too many firsts left in the world. I had always wanted to do a big expedition and a first. I wanted to travel through the Arctic by dog team, and I wanted to be in *National Geographic.* Those were the dreams I had." Ann didn't mention that if the team reached its goal, she would be the first woman to make it to the North Pole by dogsled.

Ann Bancroft shortly before the beginning of the Steger International Polar Expedition.

When Ann heard that she had been chosen for the expedition, she immediately quit her teaching job at the Clara Barton Open School. She was the only woman asked to join the team, and as Will Steger said, "If you have one woman with seven men, the woman has to be special." The other team members were Will Steger and Paul Schurke of Minnesota, Bob Mantell and Geoff Carroll from Alaska, Brent Boddy and Richard Weber from Canada, and Bob McKerrow from New Zealand.

In October 1985, Ann started training for the trip in Ely, Minnesota. The team members lived in tents in the woods with no running water and no electricity. They hauled water and firewood and learned how to travel by dogsled.

Each team member had particular responsibilities. Ann would take charge of first aid for both the dogs and the team, photography for the National

Deborah Bancroft visits her daughter while Ann trains for the polar expedition.

Geographic Society, and movie photography. She had learned some of her photographic skills from her father, who is a free-lance photographer.

In January 1986, the team left Ely to train on land that was closer to what they would experience on the polar ice cap—Frobisher Bay on Baffin Island in the Northwest Territories of Canada. Here they worked with the forty-nine huskies that would pull the five 1,350-pound sleds to the Pole.

Each person had a special "polar suit" that was designed to let body moisture evaporate on the outside of the clothing. That way everyone would stay dry inside the clothing. Once they were in these suits, the team members did not get out of them—not even to sleep. They also had boots, or mukluks, made out of sealskin and moosehide.

The team's diet was planned especially for the expedition. Ann and the others had a 7,000-calorie-a-day diet of oatmeal, noodles, cheese, butter, high-energy nut bars, and pemmican (a mixture of dried beef and fat). The dogs also ate pemmican, along with a special dog food. All food was carried on the huge sleds, and as it was used, the loads became lighter and easier to manage.

During the first week of March, the team and all supplies were airlifted from Frobisher Bay to the expedition's starting point on Ward Hunt Island. This barren, frozen place is the last bit of land in North America. On the arctic ice, the team was 500 miles from the nearest telephone, 900 miles from the nearest town, and 500 miles from their goal—the North Pole.

When Ann arrived on Ward Hunt Island in the dull gray light of evening, the temperature was -65° F, and the wind made it feel even colder. The next morning, March 8, the team started for the Pole, using mainly a sextant—a device that is used to calculate latitude and longitude by the sun and stars—to find their way across the forbidding icy sea.

As the sun colors the arctic sky, a sled from the Steger expedition crosses the ice.

4

North to the Pole

"The beginning," said Ann, "was a big flat expanse for one mile. We thought we'd whip that off, no problem. It didn't happen. Cold, cold temperatures and heavy sleds created so much friction between sled runners and ice that we didn't move. It was like pushing sleds through sand. At the end of a day's work, we had only gone one mile."

Keeping warm was one of the biggest challenges of the trip. During the first week, temperatures dropped to a bone-chilling -70°F. After one cold and windy day, Ann put her hand to her face and felt nothing but cardboard. She had frozen the entire left side of her face. At night, moisture froze inside the sleeping bags, and the team members had to beat their bags with crowbars to break up the chunks of ice.

The team soon felt the power of the Arctic Ocean. On March 15, the team's eighth day on the ice, the polar sea erupted in a mighty ice quake. Ann and Geoff Carroll were far behind the others when it happened. "We heard a sound like screaming wind or rushing water," she recalled. "The ice I was standing on felt like it would open up into a raging stream."

They started pushing the sled hard, and climbed onto a pressure ridge to see what was happening. From there, said Ann, the ice was lifting up "as if a giant mole were going through under the surface."

The movement of the ice and the bitter cold constantly threatened the expedition. One team member, Bob McKerrow, was injured while trying to push a sled over a pressure ridge. He had to leave by

Team members push and pull one of the sleds over a pressure ridge.

plane, along with several dogs that were no longer needed by the team.

Despite the hardships, the seven remaining members of the expedition moved forward. By April 2, the twenty-sixth day on the ice, the team had traveled 100 miles. With each passing day, the Arctic was changing. The sun no longer set on the horizon, and more sun produced more warmth. Unfortunately, the warmth began to melt the ice and form patches of open water, called leads.

To cross leads, the team members sometimes built floating ice bridges by throwing big chunks of ice into the water. Another method was to throw the dogs across a narrow lead, and then jump over themselves. At other times they used a large chunk of ice as a raft.

Crossing the leads became a contest. The team members would create an imaginary panel of judges and judge each dog team and sled on its crossing. Ann said, "It is real important to laugh at yourself and with each other when you're doing things that are hard."

As the team came closer and closer to the Pole, fewer dogs were needed. By the thirty-fifth day of the expedition, three sleds and twenty-eight dogs were left. Since the remaining three sleds were almost as heavy as they were in the beginning, their progress slowed. To lighten sleds, team members left behind iced-up parkas, sleeping bags, and equipment. For the rest of the trip, they zipped four single bags into two double bags, and slept three people to a bag.

Lighter sleds made it possible for the team to travel twenty miles a day. Racing to the Pole became important because the warmer weather of the arctic spring would soon create too many leads to cross. In mid-April Ann fell into the icy water of one lead.

Ann pulled through with courage and calm, but she was in danger of hypothermia. "I was lucky we were sleeping three people to one sleeping bag. I would not have made it through that first night by myself," she said.

Two days after Ann's plunge, Bob Mantell left the ice because his frozen toes had become too painful. That left twenty-one dogs, three sleds, and six team members to continue the journey. By the fifty-first day, they were less than 100 miles from the Pole, but no one could be sure that they would make it.

During a whiteout—a weather condition with blowing snow in which the horizon cannot be seen—the team strayed off course. The experienced explorers should have waited until it was possible to see. But they were so close to their goal that they traveled anyway—six miles west instead of north.

On the morning of May 1, day fifty-five of the

Dressed in her polar suit, Ann Bancroft sits by a sled with a sled dog.

Two team members at a camp during the expedition.

expedition, the team was twenty miles from the Pole. Everyone was giddy with excitement. "We felt like kids on a spring day, just having a good time outside," Ann recalled. "We just happened to be on top of the world."

That night, as the team members camped, Paul

Schurke stayed up late and took several sextant readings to determine their latitude and longitude. All were the same—they were at the North Pole! Ann had made it; she was the first woman to travel by dogsled to the Pole.

Though they had reached their goal, it took until seven o'clock the next evening to share the news with the outside world. They were so far away from civilization that for a while no one heard their radio message.

Finally, on May 3, three planes, full of reporters with microphones and cameras, flew to the Pole. For an hour, everyone celebrated on the ice. Then Ann read the team's statement, prepared by Paul Schurke, to the press, "We, six adventurers from different parts of the world standing where the lines of longitude of all countries meet, believe this journey stands for hope. Hope that other seemingly impossible goals

Ann Bancroft (left) and the remaining members of the Steger expedition hold up the American flag at the North Pole.

can be met by people everywhere.''

For the last time, the team folded up their tents, collected their kettles and stoves, and walked to the waiting planes. Ann felt reluctant to leave. "All this time we'd been thinking, 'I can't wait to get home.' And then it was about to disappear. I wanted to hang onto it another moment and I knew I wasn't going to. I looked out; it was gorgeous in every direction. I knew if I ever came back, it wouldn't be quite the same. I was experiencing something I'd never experience again.''

The team returned to cheering crowds in Minnesota's Twin Cities. At the airport, Ann said, "You allowed us to chase a dream. I thank you for that.'' The team members held press conferences in New York and Washington, D.C., and were recognized for their accomplishments by the United States Senate.

Ann herself won many awards. Regina High

School in Minneapolis named her Woman of the Year, and she was one of twelve Women of the Year chosen by *Ms.* magazine in December 1986. The Lab School of Washington presented her with the Outstanding Learning Disabled Achiever Award for serving as a role model for thousands of learning disabled students around the country.

Although Ann did not return to her teaching job after her journey to the North Pole, she believes that she has continued her work in education through public speaking and volunteer activities. Speaking about her polar adventure has enabled Ann to travel to almost every U.S. state and even to Italy.

Outside of public speaking jobs, her volunteer work keeps her busy. Among other charities, Ann is involved with Wilderness Inquiry, a nonprofit organization that introduces able and disabled people to the wilderness. Groups from this organization travel

At the airport in Minnesota's Twin Cities, Ann is welcomed by cheering crowds.

Ann Bancroft talks about her polar adventure with students at Saint James School, where she had once been a physical education teacher and athletic director.

to wilderness areas in such places as northern Minnesota, Canada, and Australia for two to three weeks at a time.

Ann continues to challenge herself in all areas of her life. One goal she considers perhaps even more difficult for her than the trip to the Pole—writing a book about her adventures.

But Ann hopes to meet other challenges, too, including an all-women's dogsled expedition. In the future, her determined will to succeed and her strong spirit of adventure will lead her to try to fulfill many more goals and dreams.

Famous Arctic Expeditions

1905   Admiral Robert E. Peary and his crew sail on the *Roosevelt* to Ellesmere Island, near Greenland. There, they leave the ship and travel by dogsled toward the pole. Peary and his crew are forced to turn back two hundred miles from the North Pole.

1908   Once again, Peary travels on dogsleds from Ellesmere Island. Most of his party turn back due to lack of supplies and bad weather. Peary is left with his assistant, Matthew Henson, and four crew members.

1909   In April, Dr. Frederick A. Cook sends a cablegram: "Reached North Pole April 21, 1908." Most historians do not believe Cook actually reached the Pole during his arctic expedition. A few days later, Peary sends a cable, saying "I have the Pole, April 6, 1909." For many years history books call Peary the first person to reach the North Pole. Recently discovered navigational notes, though, have raised doubts that Peary actually reached the Pole.

1926   Admiral Robert E. Byrd and a crew of fifty sail to northern Greenland. After setting up camp, Byrd and the crew prepare the plane, *Josephine Ford*, which Byrd plans to use to fly over the North Pole. Work is finished on May 9. Admiral Byrd and his mechanic, Floyd Bennett, take off from the top of a hill and soon discover there is a leak in the engine. Despite this, the plane reaches the North Pole and returns safely to Greenland.

    Three days later, Norwegian explorer Roald Amundsen passes over the pole in the dirigible, *Norge*.

1957   The nuclear-powered submarine, *Nautilus*, leaves its dock in Seattle. Commander William Anderson of the U.S. Navy plans to journey to the North Pole beneath the ice. However, as the submarine sails closer to the North Pole, the gyroscope breaks, forcing the team to turn back. They have succeeded in going farther north than any other ship.

1958   In the spring, the *Nautilus* and its crew again attempt to sail under the arctic ice cap, this time from west to east. The submarine crosses the Bering Strait beneath the ice and begins moving farther north. The ice soon becomes too thick, though, and they are forced to turn back.

In July, the *Nautilus* makes its third trip. The submarine submerges off Point Barrow, Alaska, and heads north. On August 3, the *Nautilus* reaches the North Pole, establishing a northern passage between the Pacific and Atlantic oceans.

1968   The Ralph Plaisted Expedition, made up of a team of four, becomes the first group to reach the North Pole by snowmobile on April 19.

1978   Naomi Uemeri, a Japanese explorer, becomes the first person to travel alone by dogsled to the North Pole.

1986 The Steger International Polar Expedition, made up of seven men and one woman, leaves northern Canada on March 6. Two members are forced to turn back due to injuries.

On the fifty-fifth day of the expedition, the remaining six team members decide to stop for the night. They awake on the morning of May 2 to discover they have camped within two hundred yards of the North Pole. The Steger International Polar Expedition becomes the first to complete a confirmed dogsled journey to the North Pole without resupply. Ann Bancroft becomes the first woman to reach the pole by dogsled.

Index

food for, 40; members of,
12, 35, 38, 39, 44, 49,
51; at the North Pole, 51;
temperatures during, 43;
training for, 38, 39-40
Twin Cities, 53
U.S. Senate, 53

University of Oregon, 26,
28
University of Wyoming, 25
Ward Hunt Island, 41
Washington, D.C., 53
whiteout, 49
Wilderness Inquiry, 55

About the Author

Dorothy Wenzel, a Minneapolis-based free-lance writer, believes that Ann Bancroft is an excellent role model for young people with disabilities, as well as able-bodied individuals. To prepare for writing this biography, Ms. Wenzel interviewed Ann Bancroft and her mother at length and read the many accounts of the expedition to the North Pole. The author has been a long-time elementary school librarian and is a member of the Society of Children's Book Writers.